Little People, BIG DREAMS

JANE AUSTEN

Written by
Mª Isabel Sánchez Vegara

Illustrated by
Katie Wilson

Lincoln
Children's Books

The Austen family lived in the heart of the English countryside. Every evening, there were eight children seated at the table for dinner: James, George, Edward, Henry, Francis, Charles, Cassandra…

...and little Jane!

At that time, girls were only allowed to do things like singing, sewing, and housework. Jane and her sister, Cassandra, found being a girl a bit of a pain.

However, Jane's father ran a school and taught the sons of wealthy men. One day, he asked his daughters to join their classes and learn the same things as the boys.

Jane loved to read. She always chose
a book instead of her dolls and spent
endless hours in her parents' library.

Jane and her siblings would often write and perform their own plays. She came up with the best stories and soon realized she wanted to become a writer!

Every night, her seven brothers and sisters sat around the fireplace. They loved listening to Jane's stories until it was time to go to bed.

One evening, Jane was at a ball and met a young man named Tom. As they talked, they fell more and more in love with each other.

But Tom's family thought Jane wasn't good enough for their son. And instead of fighting for what he wanted, he proposed to a rich heiress to please his family.

Jane decided to write a similar story to this,
but with a much happier ending. And so,
the novel *Pride and Prejudice* was born.
A daring girl named Lizzy was its heroine.

Jane kept on writing about young women who were brave enough to make their own choices and who never gave up.

MARIANNE

FANNY

ELIZABETH

When her first book came out, many people loved it.
But Jane decided to keep her name a secret.

BY
A LADY

Jane went on to write seven novels full of grace and talent. Little did she know that, one day, she would be considered one of the greatest writers in the world.

Little Jane would be happy that the books she once
wrote are the ones we still love reading today.

JANE AUSTEN

(Born 1775 • Died 1817)

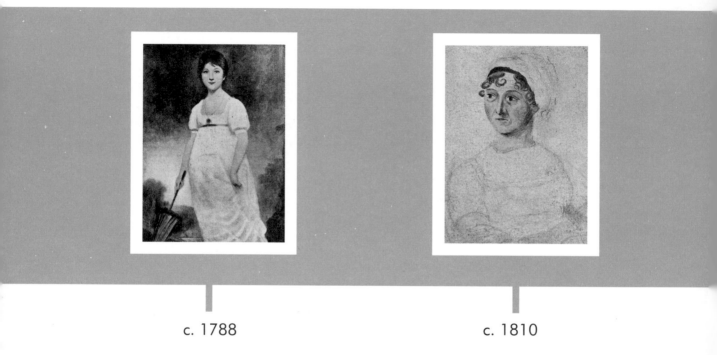

c. 1788   c. 1810

Jane Austen was born in Steventon, in England. As the seventh of eight children, she grew up in a very large family with six brothers and one sister. She was extremely close to her only sister, Cassandra, for her whole life. Her family valued learning, and Jane went to boarding school. She received a limited education but had to return home due to sickness. She was then educated at home by her father. It was in these early years that her love of reading and writing began. She wrote poems, plays, and stories, and then her first work, *Love and Friendship*, at the age of 14. It poked fun at the overdramatic novels that were popular at the

19th century   2017

time and showed her clear talent for language. Jane continued writing and authored seven very famous novels including *Sense and Sensibility, Pride and Prejudice, Emma,* and *Persuasion.* They all offered witty insights into the lives of the landed gentry at that time. Jane published her books anonymously under the name "A. Lady," and it wasn't until after her death that she was recognized for her talent. Now her works are rarely out of print or off the television screen. Although she received a proposal, Jane chose not to marry. She lived a happy life surrounded by family. To this day, she remains one of the world's most beloved writers.

Want to find out more about **Jane Austen?**
Read one of these great books:

Search and Find: Pride & Prejudice by Sarah Powell and Amanda Enright
Where's Jane? by Rebecca Smith and Katy Dockrill
Who Was Jane Austen? by Sarah Fabiny
Pride and Prejudice retold by Susanna Davidson and Simona Bursi

If you're in England, you could even visit Jane Austen's House Museum—where
Jane lived and wrote her bestselling books.

Brimming with creative inspiration, how-to projects, and useful
information to enrich your everyday life, Quarto Knows is a favorite
destination for those pursuing their interests and passions. Visit our
site and dig deeper with our books into your area of interest:
Quarto Creates, Quarto Cooks, Quarto Homes, Quarto Lives,
Quarto Drives, Quarto Explores, Quarto Gifts, or Quarto Kids.

Text © 2018 Mª Isabel Sánchez Vegara. Illustrations © 2018 Katie Wilson.

First Published in the U.S.A. in 2018 by Lincoln Children's Books, an imprint of The Quarto Group.
400 First Avenue North, Suite 400, Minneapolis, MN 55401, USA.
T (612) 344-8100 F (612) 344-8692 **www.QuartoKnows.com**
First Published in Spain in 2018 under the title Pequeña & Grande Jane Austen
by Alba Editorial, s.l.u., Baixada de Sant Miquel, 1, 08002 Barcelona
www.albaeditorial.es
All rights reserved.
Published by arrangement with Alba Editorial, s.l.u. Translation rights arranged by IMC Agència Literària, SL
All rights reserved.

A catalog record for this book is available from the British Library.
ISBN 978-1-78603-120-4
The illustrations were created with watercolor, gouache, colored pencils, and digital techniques. Set in Futura BT.

Published by Rachel Williams • Designed by Karissa Santos
Edited by Katy Flint • Production by Jenny Cundill

Manufactured in Guangdong, China CC052018

9 8 7 6 5 4 3 2 1

Photographic acknowledgments (pages 28–29, from left to right) 1. Jane Austen—portrait of the English novelist as a young woman, from the
painting by Ozias Humphry © Lebrecht Music and Arts Photo Libray / Alamy 2. Jane Austen (1775–1817) pencil and watercolor by her sister,
Cassandra Austen, c. 1810 © Granger Historical Picture Archive / Alamy 3. Jane Austen stipple engraving, 19th century © Granger Historical
Picture Archive / Alamy 4. The new 2017 Polymer ten-pound banknote, 2017 © Malcolm Haines / Alamy

Also in the *Little People,* **BIG DREAMS** series:

FRIDA KAHLO

ISBN: 978-1-84780-783-0

Meet Frida Kahlo, one of the best artists of the twentieth century.

COCO CHANEL

ISBN: 978-1-84780-784-7

Discover the life of Coco Chanel, the famous fashion designer.

MAYA ANGELOU

ISBN: 978-1-84780-889-9

Read about Maya Angelou—one of the world's most beloved writers.

AMELIA EARHART

ISBN: 978-1-84780-888-2

Learn about Amelia Earhart—the first female to fly solo over the Atlantic.

AGATHA CHRISTIE

ISBN: 978-1-78603-220-1

Meet the queen of the imaginative mystery—Agatha Christie.

MARIE CURIE

ISBN: 978-1-84780-962-9

Be introduced to Marie Curie, the Nobel Prize–winning scientist.

ROSA PARKS

ISBN: 978-1-78603-018-4

Discover the life of Rosa Parks, the first lady of the civil rights movement.

AUDREY HEPBURN

ISBN: 978-1-78603-053-5

Learn about the iconic actress and humanitarian—Audrey Hepburn.

EMMELINE PANKHURST

ISBN: 978-1-78603-020-7

Meet Emmeline Pankhurst, the suffragette who helped women get the vote.

ELLA FITZGERALD

ISBN: 978-1-78603-087-0

Meet Ella Fitzgerald, the pioneering jazz singer and musician.

ADA LOVELACE
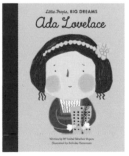

ISBN: 978-1-78603-076-4

Read all about Ada Lovelace, the first computer programmer.

GEORGIA O'KEEFFE

ISBN: 978-1-78603-122-8

Discover the life of Georgia O'Keeffe, the famous American painter.

HARRIET TUBMAN

ISBN: 978-1-78603-227-0

Learn about Harriet Tubman, who led hundreds of slaves to freedom.